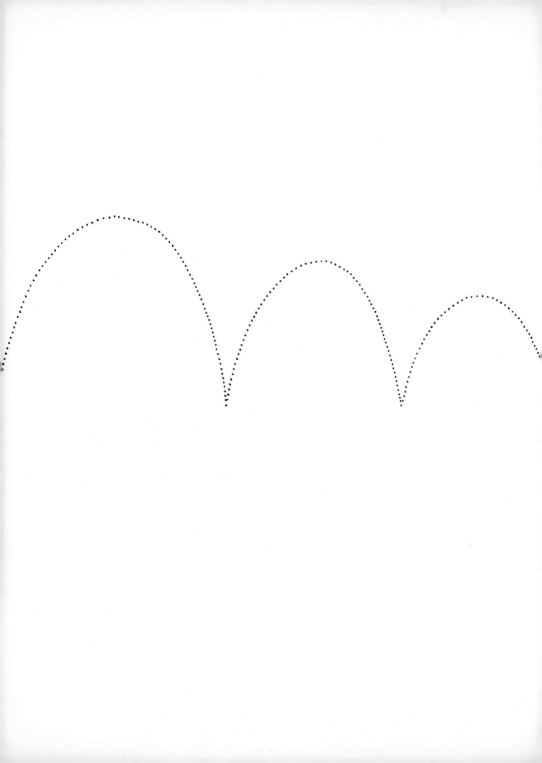

That's the Way the Ball Bounces

Gene Elston

Design and Illustration by Roland Rodegast

Published by The C. R. Gibson Company
Norwalk, Connecticut

to Anne
for her interest
and care

Copyright © MCMLXXI by
The C. R. Gibson Company, Norwalk, Connecticut
All rights reserved
Printed in the United States
Library of Congress Catalog Card Number: 78-148611
SBN: 8378-1720-X

Sports personalities are too often pictured as completely serious competitors, "giving their all" for the game. While sports naturally involves a very serious attitude, there is also a lighter side which fans are seldom aware of.

I think you will find this intriguing collection of sports humor and wit constitutes one of the most enjoyable, amusing and refreshing books it will ever be your pleasure to read.

"That's The Way The Ball Bounces" will be a welcome addition to any sports' library.

WARREN C. GILES, PRESIDENT EMERITUS
THE NATIONAL LEAGUE OF PROFESSIONAL BASEBALL CLUBS

You Win Some and You Lose Some!

Hollis Thurston, whose nickname was "Sloppy," could hardly have been called sloppy when he won 20 games for the Chicago White Sox in 1924. Thurston had reason to consider this a remarkable feat, inasmuch as the White Sox finished last in the American League that year, and he was convinced his 20 wins would provide him with a strong selling point in requesting a raise for the next season. During the winter, Sloppy wrote a letter to the club, asking for a substantial increase in salary and added, "Don't forget I won 20 games for a last-place club." Back came this telegram from the White Sox: "No raise. We could have finished last without you!"

Second Thought!

One of the most popular underground films, witnessed only by a privileged few, has been put together by Hank Stram, coach of the Kansas City Chiefs football team. It contains eight minutes of 'clips' from free-for-alls his club has been involved in through the years. One of the biggest laugh-getters is a sequence featuring Bobby Ply, first shown standing on the sidelines as a brawl breaks out on the field. The following scenes show Ply rushing toward the action, stopping suddenly, running back to the bench — and quickly donning his helmet before dashing back into the midst of the fist-swinging players! Stram calls the movie, naturally, "Greatest Fights of the Century."

Instant Pollution!

At St. Andrews Golf Course in Scotland, a lovely little brook — the Swilcan Burn — winds through and crosses the first and eighteenth holes. Andrew Kirkaldy, long-time pro for this Royal and Ancient Club, teed off one morning, drove just short of the Burn and pitched his second shot within inches of the hole. It seemed a fine day as he and his partner crossed the pretty little rustic bridge that led to the green. "John," he said happily, "often as I pass this way, I never tire of looking at the lovely Swilcan Burn. With its green, grassy banks and the clear water running over the white pebbles, it's one of the prettiest little streams in all of Scotland."

Everything went well until the eighteenth, when he hit a rank topper off the tee that skittered down the fairway — and into the rippling Swilcan Burn. Kirkaldy strode hopefully to the edge of the brook, but there lay his ball among the white pebbles in six inches of water. "Caddie," he bellowed, "quit standing there gaping and fetch my ball out of that damned dirty little ditch!"

The Last Word!

As a referee in the National Basketball Association many years ago, Sid Borgia looked like a midget alongside most of the players. Borgia stood only 5 feet 8 inches and weighed 140 pounds.

Once, during a hotly contested game, Borgia called a personal and then a technical foul on Ed Sadowski, who towered over Sid at 6 feet 8 inches. The calls so enraged Sadowski that he grabbed Borgia by the shirt-front, lifted him up and bellowed, "Borgia, I'm going to kill you!" Gasping for air, the game little referee huffed, "Ed, before I die, I want you to know there's another technical coming up!"

The Camera Never Lies!

Sports' officials are generally agreed that to succeed in their profession it helps to have, among other things, a good sense of humor and great physical stamina. A man who seems to have an abundance of both is Bill Valentine, who spends his summers as an American League baseball umpire and his winters officiating college basketball. It was during a basketball game that Valentine had a head-on collision with one of the players. A photographer caught them at the exact moment of impact. Next day, the picture appeared in a local paper, along with a caption which so amused the bruised official that he bought extra copies to send to his friends. The caption over the picture read: "Valentine hit from the blind side — right between the eyes!"

Floor-cast!

Possibly one of the most prophetic pieces of advice ever expressed was written unwittingly by a school teacher of Joe Louis, the young man who was later to become heavyweight boxing champion of the world. The teacher was making a routine evaluation of her pupils, with the purpose of advising whether they should go on to prepare for college or take high school training in the manual trades. When the teacher came to Louis' name, she wrote: "This boy should certainly learn to do something with his hands."

Rah Recruits!

When colleges and universities conclude their football seasons, the recruiting of high school athletes becomes a full-time job. The competition has grown more intense with each passing year, primarily because of the increase in the number of coaches on major college staffs, which allows more men to be out beating the bushes for new prospects.

Thus far, no one has come up with a workable solution to the problem, but a few years ago the very successful former head mentor at Penn State, Rip Engle, presented his coaching colleagues with the most practical — and unique — recruiting tip heard in a long time.

"Go out and find yourself a pair of 230-pound guards," Engle advised his associates, "and it makes no difference whether they can play!" Then Rip added, "Assign these two to carry you off the field after every game, and the alumni will say, 'Well, maybe he can't coach, but the boys certainly love him!'"

Reverse English

This is Charlie Grimm's story about the scout who telephoned him one evening while Grimm was managing the Chicago Cubs. The scout went into ecstasies about the 'greatest pitching prospect he had ever seen', describing eloquently his outstanding performance in an amateur game in Wisconsin. "This boy," the scout raved on, "has speed, control, a great curve — everything! He struck out all 27 men to face him, and only one of them even hit a foul ball off him!" Grimm, whose Cubs' collective batting average had been a matter of dismal concern all year, broke in with equal enthusiasm! "What we need are hitters," he exclaimed. "Go sign the player who hit that foul ball!"

Salute!

During his successful career as football coach at Florida University, Bob Woodruff was standing on the sidelines one afternoon, watching his team work out. He was puffing on a cigar and chatting with Phil Dickens, his former Tennessee teammate, when suddenly there was a lull in the conversation as both men glanced up to see their old coach, the formidable General Bob Neyland, approaching them. Instinctively, Woodruff tossed away his cigar. Dickens looked at his friend in astonishment and asked, "What did you do that for, Bob? He isn't your boss any more!" "I know that," Woodruff replied, "but I'm not sure HE does!"

'Foot-in-Mouth' Disease!

Chances are "The Bartered Bride" would not be included among Sparky Stalcup's favorite works of music — and with good reason! Prior to assuming his new position as assistant athletic director at Missouri, Sparky had a long and occasionally frustrating career as basketball coach of the Tigers. One night, after a particularly tough defeat, Stalcup was still fuming when he returned home. His wife, trying to comfort him, remarked, "That's all right, dear. Don't worry about it. You still have me." Whereupon the "net" results of a disastrous evening proved too much for Sparky to resist. "Yes," said the fearless coach, "and I'm glad I still have you . . . but there were times tonight when I would have gladly traded you for a basket!"

Pay Attention!

When Anne Hayes, wife of Ohio State's football coach, Woody Hayes, had a point to make, she could be as outspoken as her famous husband, and during a recent speaking engagement her candid remarks had the crowd roaring. At the conclusion of her speech, someone in the audience asked a question about Woody's latest book on football, and Mrs. Hayes' eyes sparkled.

"I haven't had a thing to do with the new book," she said emphatically, "and what's more I won't!" Then she explained, "When Woody's first book was published in 1957, we handled everything ourselves. You can imagine what happened. We had football books all over the place — couldn't even get the car in the garage. To top that off, I ended up doing all the mailing and just about everything else! Finally, when he started writing the new book, I went to Woody and told him: 'After seven years, I'm still not getting a cent for this! You might say I've been doing it for love — and lately I'm not getting any of that, either!' So I just up and quit, and he couldn't get me to tackle that job again for love *nor* money!"

"Unaccustomed as I Am . . ."

Joe Dugan, who played third base for the Yankees when Babe Ruth was at his immortal best, loved to tell of the time Ruth shook hands with President Warren Harding. It was before a game in Washington, with the thermometer hovering around the 90-degree mark, when they learned the President was in attendance and wanted to meet some of the players. Dugan said he advised Ruth to be prepared to say a few words to the President when he was introduced. "The rest of us will just shake hands," Dugan told the Babe, "but you're a big-shot. You're expected to make a remark!" Undaunted, when the introductions began, Ruth walked up to Harding, stuck out his hand and growled, "Hotter'n hell out here today, eh, Prez?"

Nobody's Perfect!

Following the National League expansion, when the New York Mets began their desperate search for baseball talent, Manager Casey Stengel helped conduct one of their tryout camps for young hopefuls. Stengel noted that one boy was wearing shinguards, so Casey invited the young man to get behind the plate and show what he could do. The boy protested that he wasn't a catcher — he was an infielder. Naturally, Stengel wanted to know why the kid was wearing shinguards if he was trying out for the infield. "Well," said the boy, "I'm a little weak on ground balls!"

Better Luck Next Time!

Lefty Gomez was a very young ballplayer from a very small town the day he almost got into his first major league game being played before some 70,000 fans!

It was at Yankee Stadium, and Herb Pennock was pitching for New York with Gomez out in the bullpen, praying Pennock had his stuff. All went well until the 8th inning when Pennock, after striking out the first batter, gave up a single

Punch-Line!

During a *bout* between boxers Otto Sealoff and Chappy Jones many years *ago*, Jones was taking a terrible drubbing. Suddenly Sealoff connected with a hard right to the jaw, and Chappy *went* down. Referee George Siler bent over the fallen boxer and *began* his count. As the referee reached the toll of six, he noticed that Chappy's eyes were open. Siler delayed his next count for a moment, pausing to ask Jones, "Do you intend to fight any more?" "Yes, sir, Mr. Siler," Chappy said softly. "I intend to fight some more — but not tonight."

Write or Wrong!

Credit Joe Namath, the outstanding quarterback for the New York Jets — and the Toast of Broadway during the '60's — with having a wit as quick as his passing arm! Having been needled steadily by a New York sportswriter concerning Joe's checkered classroom career at Alabama, Namath was finally asked sarcastically, "What DID you major in, Joe? Basket-weaving?" Namath shook his head and, with a reasonably straight face, answered, "No, I found basket-weaving was too tough, so I switched to Journalism!"

Epitaph!

Frankie Frisch, who led the Cardinals' notorious Gas House Gang of the 1930's, was honored at the 1968 World Series by being selected to throw out the first ball for one of the games. An equally distinguished Series' visitor that year was Casey Stengel, with whom Frisch had long carried on a mock feud while both men were managers in the National League. Reminiscing, the two of them recalled the time when Stengel, then managing the woefully weak Boston Braves, suffered a broken leg after being hit by a taxicab. The first telegram to reach him at the hospital was from Frisch. It read: "Your unsuccessful attempt to commit suicide is deeply lamented."

and walked the following batter. The next man up sent a screaming line drive back to the mound that hit Herb on the knee. Manager Bob Shawkey called time, went out to talk to Pennock and finally signalled to the umpire to bring in Gomez. It was a long walk from the bullpen, and it seemed even longer that day. All kinds of thoughts went through Gomez' mind as he got closer to making his major league debut. As he walked those last few steps to the mound where Pennock and Shawkey were still standing, he tried to appear composed. "How should I pitch to this first batter, Skip?" he croaked. Shawkey stared at him, then blurted out, "Hell, kid, I don't want you to pitch! Pennock broke the webbing in his glove. Just give him yours and get back to the bullpen!"

It Figures!

Max Baer, former heavyweight boxing champion, was a carefree, happy-go-lucky guy who spent his money as fast as he won it — sometimes faster. Whenever Baer needed extra money, he would simply sell someone another percentage of his contract, until it was suddenly discovered that Max had oversold himself — to the tune of 125%!

Baer's attorney was summoned to talk to Max and to try to explain the situation to his irate shareholders. "Max," the lawyer began, "How could you possibly sell 25% that doesn't exist?"

"Why," Baer countered innocently, "all the people who own part of my contract keep telling me I've got to put out ONE-THOUSAND per cent!"

Be My Guest

Probably the most lopsided college football score ever recorded was Georgia Tech's victory over Cumberland in 1916 — 222 to 0! The beleaguered Cumberland quarterback was a fellow named George Allen. Quarterback Allen used to recall just one of the many times he fumbled in the face of Georgia

Tech's intimidating onslaught that day. This time, as the ball bounced away, Allen saw three Tech giants bearing down on it — and him! George yelled to a nearby teammate, "Pick it up!" Instead, the unhappy teammate veered the other way, shouting, "YOU pick it up — I didn't drop it!"

Hidden Meaning!

Two-Ton Tony Galento, who campaigned as a heavyweight fighter with mixed success for many years, once became irritated with a New York sportswriter, Cas Adams, and threatened to throw the newspaperman out of his training camp.

"You ain't welcome here," Galento snarled at the writer. "I don't like them things you been sayin' about me." Adams, undismayed, replied briskly, "I wrote that you were a bum — and I reiterate it!"

Galento's chubby face lit up, and he clapped Adams on the shoulder. "Well, that's different," he said happily, "I accept your apology!"

Fore Runner!

The gaudy garb sported by many of the bright young golf pros today has generally become accepted as a matter of 'course'. Yet the attire worn by these brilliant golfers would hardly have lent more color to the game than did that of Adam Green, a popular swinger of the early 1900's.

Green, displaying courage as well as colorful taste, must have created a loud 'hue' and cry among his competitors when he appeared on the links. He played regularly in patent-leather shoes, topped by spats, and wore a brightly checked jacket over a shirt with sparkling celluloid collar and cuffs. Green knickers and red gloves completed his colorful raiment, but the resplendent golfer added to the unusual effect by donning goggles for driving off the tee — after which he switched to a monocle!

Lee's Revenge!

In the late 1920's, the University of Mississippi two brothers enrolled, Ge and Harvey Walker. Bot were being sought after by several major league baseball clubs. The brot received their best offer the New York Yankees were almost ready to a However, before signin contracts, they decide discuss the offer with mother, an unreconst Rebel. Her Confeder proved too much for New York organizat she vowed, "No son will ever wear a Ya uniform!" They did Both boys eventua with the Detroit T whose flag Harvey part-time through — while Gee turn to be a whiz!

Just in Time!

In 1959, Murray Warmath's University of Minnesota football team had such a pitiful record that the local fans hanged him in effigy and dumped garbage on his lawn. The next season, however, his Gophers lost just one game, won the Big Ten Championship and went on to the Rose Bowl.

Suddenly Coach Warmath was flooded with praise instead of censure. One jubilant fan was prompted to write a letter which Murray treasures. Said the fan: "Mr. Warmath, you are a great coach, and your team has come a long way. You are a heck of a lot better coach than we had last year!"

Hold That Line!

Kentucky's Adolph Rupp, who has won more games than any other college basketball coach, has never been a man to take victory for granted, no matter what the score! One time when his Kentucky team jumped off to a commanding lead of something like 40 to 3 against a small college in Arkansas, Rupp called time out and demanded, "Who's supposed to be covering that Number 12 — the one who's been scoring all their points?" Guard Ralph Beard spoke right up. "He's my man, Coach," said Beard. "Well, get on him!" Rupp shouted. "That rascal is going hog wild!"

Baseball Buff!

Baseball players, like most athletes, have long been known for coming up with new alibis for their mistakes. However, one of the old ones still stands out as a 'shining' example! Josh Devore, an old-time outfielder for the New York Giants, was prepared with a unique alibi after he dropped a high fly ball at a critical point in the game. When the inning was over, Devore hastened over to Manager John McGraw and explained, "I had a manicure this morning, and I was momentarily blinded by the reflection of the sun on my fingernails!"

Sea-ing Is Believing!

Norman Ross, a champion long-distance swimmer, had paddled far out into Lake Michigan from a Chicago beach for practice. When he neared the shore on his return, he saw that a large crowd had gathered. Having appeared 'out of the blue' on previous occasions, Ross was not looking forward to the barrage of silly questions he was sure to be asked when he landed. As he reached shallow water, Ross stood up and shouted, "What city is this?" The crowd hollered back, "Chicago." "Oh, heck," yelled Ross, "I wanted Milwaukee!" And with several hundred people gaping incredulously, he dived back into the lake and swam away.

Empathy!

At an informal gathering one evening, former New York Yankee great Joe DiMaggio was defending the extremely high salaries paid in recent years to some of baseball's heroes. During the discussion, he pointed out that a player's peak of activity was relatively short, and that even during this time he was constantly battling — and uncomfortably aware of — the inroads of age. Joe went on to point out that with younger competition breathing down his neck, it was imperative for each player to make the most of his limited time at the top. Listening without a trace of sympathy was Mrs. Paul Gallico, wife of the famous author. "Now," she said, "you begin to have *some* idea of how it feels to be a woman!"

Hoot, Mon!

Bobby Jones, the greatest of amateur golfers, was always impressed by the experience, wisdom and dignity of the caddies — many of them old men — at the famous St. Andrews Course in Scotland. He recalls one ancient caddy, a nimble-witted Scotsman of over 70 years, who one year got stuck with a very poor — and extremely unpleasant — golfer for the British Amateur Tournament. From the beginning, the golfer found fault with everything the caddy did, blaming him for all of his problems, including his own shortcomings as a golfer. Finally, after a particularly bad round, he turned and snapped, "I have drawn the worst caddy in the world!" With a wry smile the old man replied, "Oh, no, sir. That would be quite *too* great a coincidence."

Hands Off!

With two minutes remaining in a game being played in the rain against Lock Haven State College, John Huntey was calling signals in a mud-streaked uniform for Waynesburg College. His team was facing a last-ditch effort to hold on to a slim 14-13 lead, and the quarterback also knew he would need a good grip on the football. During the preceding play, he had muddied both his hands and the towel at his waist in diving for a loose ball. Looking for a solution to the problem, his eyes lit upon the only clean places on the field — the officials' uniforms. Calmly, without asking, Huntey began to wipe his hands on the trousers of a startled field judge. Just as calmly, the affronted dignitary paced off 15 yards against Waynesburg for unsportsmanlike conduct.

Ace in the Hole?

When Bo McMillin was football coach at Indiana in the 1940's, he decided he'd have to take his star halfback down a peg or two. So it was that McMillin put Bob Hoernschemeyer, better known as "Hunchy," on the second team in a scrimmage against the regulars. The first time Hunchy got the ball, he ran 97 yards off tackle for a touchdown. Still intent on chastising his ace, McMillin pointed out all the things Hunchy had done wrong — how he had hit the wrong hole, cut the wrong way, failed to stiff-arm a halfback, and so on. Hunchy listened to everything Bo had to say, then smiled serenely and asked, "Yeah, but how was it for DISTANCE, coach?"

Grand Finale!

Umpire Shag Crawford of the National League was working second base on the day Dick Groat played his last major league game in 1967. Groat, who spent most of his baseball career with the Pittsburgh Pirates, was a scrappy ballplayer and an outstanding hitter whose skill with a bat was still evident on his last day when he singled to right-center field. In his attempt to stretch the hit into a double, he was called out on a close play at second base by Crawford.

Groat, in typical form, complained bitterly about the veteran umpire's decision, but when he left Crawford it was with the remark, "Shag, even though you missed that one, you're still the second-best umpire in the league."

Crawford was naturally flattered by what Groat had said, but equally curious to know who Dick considered number one. When the game ended, Shag caught up with Groat in the dugout tunnel and asked, "Dick, if I'm second, who's the best?" And Groat replied without hesitation, "The other 19 are tied for first!"

Catcher in the Wry!

During the 1970 World Series, Catcher Andy Etchebarren of the Orioles revealed that two other major league clubs had offered him a bigger bonus than the $85,000 he ultimately received for signing with Baltimore. One of the better offers came from Houston, where the recently organized Colt .45s were shooting for top talent to fill the gaps created by baseball's expansion.

Lum Harris, who was a coach for Baltimore Manager Paul Richards at the time Etchebarren joined the Orioles, vividly recalled his first meeting with the rookie catcher. "I asked him why he signed with Baltimore, and Andy explained it was mostly because he wanted to play for Mr. Richards," said Lum. "And I had to tell him Paul would be leaving Baltimore at the end of the season — to take over at Houston!"

Heads Up!

Wally Butts, former Georgia football coach, likes to tell of one unique method employed by Bear Bryant, the famous Alabama coach, to get his players worked up to a ferocious pitch in the pursuit and recovery of fumbles. One day, after witnessing a couple of fumbles during practice, Bryant gathered his entire squad around him in a circle, then asked a student manager to go and get a dozen footballs. As soon as the balls were piled tightly in the center of the ring of players, Bryant judiciously stepped out of the circle and bellowed, "All right . . . EVERYBODY get a ball!"

No Comprende!

One of the drawbacks of being well-known as a sports' 'personality' is that these people are generally considered 'fair game' by fans and writers alike.

One morning, a newspaperman telephoned the hotel room of Camilio Pascual, the crafty Cuban pitcher for the Washington Senators, at a very early hour. When Pascual sleepily muttered into the receiver, the inconsiderate sportswriter, intent only on getting his story, commenced the interview by inquiring unhappily, "Camilio, don't you speak English?"

"Not at 7 o'clock in the morning!" snapped Pascual, and hung up the phone.

It Makes Scents!

The National Football League once had a referee named Harry Robb — and there was a day when the Pittsburgh Steelers thought they were being robbed by Harry! The referee had penalized the Pittsburgh club time and time again.

Finally, Chuck Cherndulo, the Steelers' center, could restrain himself no longer. After an offside penalty, he blurted out, "Robb, you stink!" Without a word, Harry stepped off another 15 yards. Then the referee turned to Cherndulo and asked sweetly, "How do I smell from here, Chuck?"

Mixed-Up Kid

A minor league baseball club signed a raw young pitcher in mid-season. Before his first game, the veteran catcher discussed signals with the new recruit. "I don't want to confuse you," he said, "so today we'll just use one finger for a fast ball and two fingers for a curve." The game commenced. Eight times the catcher signaled for a fast ball, only to have the pitcher walk the first two batters on eight consecutive balls! Finally, the unhappy catcher signaled for a curve, which the rookie promptly broke in over the plate for a strike. Calling time, the catcher rushed to congratulate the young pitcher. "I was hoping you'd call for a curve," said the rookie. "It's hard to control the ball with only one finger!"

Eye, Eye, Sir!

Uncle Charlie Moran was nearing the end of a long and commendable umpiring career in the National League when he got into a rhubarb with the Chicago Cubs over a decision.

Several Cub players charged from the dugout toward Uncle Charlie, seemingly bent on tearing him to pieces in their anger. Charlie Grimm, the Cub manager, hastened out to break up the commotion. Yet it was Grimm who got the thumb from Moran. Taking a firm stand between the umpire and his players, Grimm warned, "I'll fine the first guy who dares lay a hand on this blind old man!"

Cool It, Man!

During the time Freddie Hutchinson managed Cincinnati, he was continuously annoyed by hearing players complain about the heat. Although it often was unbearable at old Crosley Field, the constant griping only served to get Hutchinson hotter under the collar. Finally, in complete irritation, he called a meeting and informed his players that the next guy he heard complaining about the heat would be fined.

Not long after the warning had been issued, Art Fowler was pitching for the Reds under a broiling sun. After six innings on the scorching mound, Fowler went back to the dugout, sprawled out, closed his eyes and moaned, "Boy, I mean it's really hot in this ball park today."

As he opened his eyes, he found himself face-to-face with a steaming Hutchinson. Without missing a beat, Fowler added, "Just the way I like it!"

Nice Comeback!

After winning two straight Big Ten football championships at Michigan State in 1966 and '67, Coach Duffy Daugherty found the going rough in 1968. His Spartans were shocked by underdog University of Houston, 37 to 7, in their opener. They won only three games all season and finally stumbled into a three-way tie for fifth place in the conference.

The following summer, a sportswriter was sounding out Daugherty on his prospects for a comeback. The writer, during the course of the interview asked Duffy, "Who are you happiest to see returning to your squad this year?" Daugherty, without a moment's hesitation, replied, "ME!"

Photo Finish!

For many years, before each World Series game, it has been traditional for the starting pitchers from each team to pose together for photographers. One pitcher who declined to honor this tradition was Lon Warneke, when he was a young star with the Chicago Cubs. It was during the 1932 Series that Warneke balked and told the battery of photographers he was sorry, but he didn't like to pose for pictures on the day he was to pitch. One of the cameramen jeered at Lon, "What's the matter? Don't tell me you're superstitious!" The young pitcher grew indignant. "Heck, no," he snapped. "I just happen to think it's unlucky!"

Looking A'head!

Following his retirement as one of the greatest of Yankee pitchers, Lefty Gomez became affiliated with a major sporting goods' company. One of his duties as their representative was to visit the various clubs during spring training and measure the players for new uniforms. An experience Gomez had with Yogi Berra literally 'capped' them all. Berra was still catching for the Yankees when Lefty got out his tape measure one early spring day to find out what size shirt and pants Yogi would need. Then, to complete his report, Gomez asked Berra what size cap he wore. "How should I know," Yogi answered. "I'm not in shape yet!"

Identity Unknown!

When Red Grange was enjoying his third year as an All-American halfback at Illinois in the 1920's, one of his greatest games was against the powerful Pennsylvania team in Philadelphia.

Despite a muddy field, Grange was running wild. He was almost the whole show. The Penn coach kept changing tackles in a vain effort to stop the Galloping Ghost. Finally he called for another substitute. His instructions were simple: "Get in there and stop Grange!"

The sub tackle trotted out onto the field, then turned and promptly raced back to the bench. "Hey, Coach," he said breathlessly, "you forgot to tell me. Which one is Grange?"

Congratulations!

It happened in 1969 in Detroit. Things weren't going very well at the time, either for Al Kaline or for the Tigers, and the race among the top clubs — including Detroit and the Minnesota Twins — was growing increasingly tight. Under the mounting pressure, Kaline struck out against Sam McDowell in a game being played with Cleveland. Al's temper flared, and when he got back to the dugout, he slammed his bat into the rack in a violent fit of anger. Unfortunately, his hand was smashed against the bat rack, too, and the blow broke one of his fingers.

With his hand in a cast, Kaline returned to the clubhouse the next day to find the following wire tacked on his locker: "Nice going, stupid!"

The friendly message was signed by two Minnesota Twins — Harmon Killebrew and Bob Allison!

Walking Encyclopedia!

Here's a story his teammates loved to tell about Babe Herman. The incident occurred during the 1934 season, when Babe was doing his stuff for the Chicago Cubs. One afternoon in the clubhouse, Herman confided to Chuck Klein that his son, who had recently started school, had begun throwing questions every night at dinner which the Babe found as difficult to solve as he did Carl Hubbell's screwball. "Well," Klein asked, "why don't you buy him an encyclopedia?" "Aw, come on," snapped the Babe, "the kid can walk to school!"

Angel in Disguise?

Charlie Moran became a major league umpire following a successful career of coaching football at Centre College, whose team's nickname was the 'Praying Colonels.' One time, during an argument with Moran over a decision, Fresco Thompson sneered, "With you as a coach, Moran, no wonder your team prayed!" Fresco recalls that Moran had the last word, however, when he turned to Thompson, smiled benignly and said, "Young man, since you've turned this conversation into religious channels, suppose you go to the clubhouse and baptize yourself with an early shower!"

Perfect Squelch!

Pete Gray was a remarkable one-armed outfielder who played for the St. Louis Browns during World War II. One sweltering day, as Gray came off the field after a strenuous game in Chicago, he was stopped by an extremely talkative woman. Caught in a 'sticky' situation, Pete tried to remain polite as the woman droned on and on about his handicap. After several uncomfortable moments, dripping with sympathy and sentimentality — to say nothing of the heat — the woman finally gushed, "You poor boy . . . just how did you lose your arm?" Pete saw his chance, and as he headed for the clubhouse he replied solemnly, "A woman in St. Louis talked it off!"

Two Heads Are Better Than None!

The unveiling of the Houston Astrodome in 1965, along with the opening of the Houston Astros' inaugural baseball season, brought newsmen from all over the country to cover events. Bill Giles, then head of Astros' Public Relations, had put in a long, hectic week when, during an exhibition game one night, an Astros' batter was hit in the face by a pitched ball. It was very late before he received a report on the player's condition, but Giles, knowing the writers had been waiting to learn the extent of the injury before filing their stories, called a hurried press conference. Bill explained that although the player would remain hospitalized for further observation, preliminary examination indicated no serious damage. One reporter asked Giles, "Do you know yet exactly where the ball hit him?" "I'm not positive," replied the weary publicist, "but from the information I received, I'd say he was hit somewhere on the left head!"

Time Out!

It's unlikely that any of the football record books contain the 'bear' facts concerning one of the most unusual goal line romps in history!

At a Baylor game in Waco, Texas, the referee threw a red flag on the ground to mark a penalty against Baylor for illegal use of hands. Just then one of Baylor's bear-cub mascots slipped out of his chained collar, dashed onto the field, grabbed the red flag and raced toward the end zone. An amused crowd watched as the bear tossed the flag in the air, batted it with a forepaw, then grabbed it again to continue his rollicking trip across the goal, before he was finally caught and carried off the field victoriously.

Nag, Nag, Nag

The seventh hole at the Santa Anita Golf Course is only a couple of brassie shots from the race track — so close, in fact, that it is possible for players to hear the race calls over the public address system. This proximity has created a mental hazard for many a golfer who enjoys playing the horses as well as the links.

On this day, however, a former jockey turned caddie, hoping to get a run for his money, had two dollars riding on a horse in the first race, while he was caddying for a man whose interests ran exclusively to the improvement of his golf game.

Reaching the seventh just as the horses were at the starting gate, the golfer made a beautiful tee shot and strode off down the fairway with the caddie following intently, his ears cocked to hear the results of the race, now entering the stretch. As they neared the ball, the golfer turned happily to ask the caddie, "What'll I use, boy?" "Your whip, you fool, your whip," hollered the caddie, "and for God's sake, be quick about it!"

Clean Hit!

A former National League pitcher, whose poor record on the mound had never affected his ego, once persuaded Rip Collins, an excellent hitter and a member of the famed "Gashouse Gang," to speak at a banquet in the pitcher's hometown. The pitcher introduced Collins and tried to impress the audience by remarking smugly, "Rip was a great batter — but he never got a hit off me in his life!" Collins recovered quickly as he stood up to acknowledge the introduction. "Yes, that's absolutely true," said Rip. "But, you see, I used to bat fifth in the order, and by the time I came up, our friend here was already in the showers!"

Sick 'em!

In 1930, several long runs made by Hank Bruder carried Northwestern to a decisive football victory over Tulane. It wasn't until two days after the game that Bruder was finally brought down — by smallpox! Northwestern authorities ordered all members of the football squad vaccinated and sent a telegram to Tulane officials advising that they do the same for their players. Bernie Bierman, the Tulane coach, wired back immediately: "It's an unnecessary precaution here. Our boys didn't get close enough to Bruder to catch him or anything else!"

Post Part 'um!

Chris Erskine, director of sports' telecasts for a Chicago station, became increasingly concerned while televising a tag-team wrestling match one night, because the combatants kept hitting the ropes on the same side of the ring, each time moving it a few inches. The TV cables, attached to one ring-post, had been pulled taut and were on the verge of breaking. Making a "snap" decision, Erskine sent an alarm to the announcer, Jack Brickhouse, who didn't need a "post script" to deal with the situation!

Brickhouse called the referee over, and the official, in turn, conversed briefly with the wrestlers. Immediately, both grapplers began hurling each other against the ropes on the other side. "Within minutes they moved the ring back where it had been," Erskine recalled, "and for the rest of the night they did a "bang-up" job of keeping us on the air!"

Guilty, Your Honor!

A number of years ago when Walter Briggs owned the Detroit Tigers, he hired a private detective to check the activities of pitcher Boots Poffenberger, well-known for his lack of concern for training rules. A few days later, Walter called Boots into start onto the field. As the band paraded off, the Oklahoma drum major threw his baton high in the air — only to drop it as it came down! Just then, a fan caught sight of Oklahoma Coach Bud Wilkinson and broke the tension when he shouted, "Hey, Bud, I see you coach the band, too!"

Tee and Sympathy!

Francis Ouimet is generally credited with giving golf in America its biggest boost toward popularity with the masses. Until Ouimet, then an obscure 20-year-old amateur, won the coveted U. S. Open in 1913, golf had been considered more of a 'social' game. Sports editors took little notice of golf events or the participants, and, if a story appeared at all, it was usually in the society section.

Years later, when Ouimet played an exhibition match in Dayton, Ohio, a local sportswriter devoted most of his feature to praising Ouimet as "the man who took golf off the society pages." Unfortunately, the sports pages were crowded with other events that day. Where did the story wind up? You guessed it — back in the society section!

What Goes Up Must Come Down!

With only a few seconds remaining in a 1970 football game between two Michigan rivals — Northern High and South-field-Lathrup — it appeared that Northern, with possession of the ball at midfield and a 12-8 lead, could not possibly lose the contest. But Quarterback Bob Chism, confident that victory was within his grasp, literally threw it away when he started "tossing" the celebration prematurely.

The clock indicated time for one more play. Chism took the snap from center and, in his exuberance, threw the ball high into the air. Unfortunately for Northern, the game was not over until the last play was completed. An alert opponent, Gary Weinberg, caught the ball and carried it 43 yards for a touchdown to "hand" Southfield-Lathrup an unexpected win!

Boys Will Be Boys!

Paul Brown never let inclement weather interfere with practice sessions when he was leading the Cleveland Browns to several pro-football championships in the 50's. One day, with the temperature at a crackling 5-below zero, Paul called his gridders out for drill. Brown's message to the shivering squad was simply, "Today we'll separate the men from the boys!" George Ratterman, a reserve quarterback, still remembers how intensely the players were suffering from the biting cold, when suddenly one of the Browns' young guards jumped out of the line of scrimmage and began trotting across the frozen field toward the warm dressing room. As he ran, he shouted back over his shoulder, "So long, MEN!"

Flaming Youth!

A fire broke out in the Iowa State University football equipment room one day just as practice ended, and all the players rushed in to help fight the blaze. Coach Clay Stapleton issued a quick order. "All you first-unit players get out of here," he roared. "The rest of you put out the fire!" When telling the story later, Stapleton added, "I didn't realize it at the time, but I must have sounded like the basketball coach whose team was asleep on the fourth floor of a hotel when a fire broke out. In the stress of the moment, he is reported to have yelled, 'First team take the fire escape . . . the rest of you jump!'"

Fumble-Bums!

Oklahoma had one of its great football teams in 1952, but a rash of fumbles plagued the Sooners during the first half of their game against Notre Dame. The players were still on edge when they came out to start the second half and found they would have to wait in the runway until the Oklahoma band concluded its rather lengthy half-time show. Palms were beginning to sweat by the time they finally got the signal to

A Wee Nip in the Air!

Willie Turnesa, an outstanding golfer of former years, was also a great student of the game. In his research, he discovered why a golf course today consists of 18 holes. Turnesa learned that in Scotland, where the game began, the number had originally varied from seven to as many as twenty-two holes, until the Board of Governors at the famed St. Andrews Course held a meeting for the purpose of establishing a uniform figure to be officially adopted. Their final decision was based on the convincing argument of one venerable Highlander, who claimed he had 'proof' from long experience that 18 nips from his bottle of Scotch — one at each tee — was exactly the proper amount of "medicine" to guard against the inclemency of the climate! — without affecting his game!

No Question About It!

Branch Rickey, during his long tenure in baseball, became known as a front office boss who demanded — and got — the healthy respect of his employees. He was a firm advocate of discipline and economy, both of which contributed to his great success as a baseball executive and did nothing to diminish his awesome reputation.

One day Rickey asked his secretary to wire an employee who had been investigating a minor league property the club was interested in acquiring, to find out whether he had closed the deal. The employee, knowing Rickey liked economy, sent his answer back in one word: "Yes."

When the telegram arrived, the office was closed and Rickey's secretary had gone for the day. The "boss," as usual, was working late, but by this time his thoughts had turned to other business. He found himself completely mystified by the terse message and without the foggiest recollection of his original query. Puzzled by the hidden meaning, Rickey wired back again, "Yes, what?"

The startled employee immediately replied, "Yes, sir!"

his office and proceeded to read off an imposing list of things the young hurler had done, as well as places he had visited. Poffenberger asked how Briggs had secured this information, and the Tiger owner admitted he had put a detective on the pitcher's heels. "That's silly," quipped Poffenberger. "You should send him after some of the other guys — you already KNOW what I'm going to do!"

First Down

Football coaches spend many hours before each season charting new plays designed to out-wit and out-maneuver their opponents, an effort requiring great mental agility and concentration. Fortunately, however, few become as engrossed in their work as a former Texas Christian coach, Francis Schmidt, once did. With his mind on football, Schmidt drove into a gas station for an oil change. While his car was lifted on the rack, the coach remained behind the wheel busily diagramming plays in a notebook. Suddenly, he hit upon a great new play. With a yell of triumph, he flung open the car door and jubilantly stepped out — and down six feet to the concrete floor! Luckily, his only injury was a sprained ankle.

Double Threat!

Don Padgett was considered a dangerous hitter when he played for the St. Louis Cardinals in the late 1930's, but Padgett was even more dangerous to his own club when he was in the field. The Cardinals' manager, Ray Blades, had tried him in the outfield, at first base and as a catcher with equally disastrous results. Wherever Padgett played, the errors piled up. Finally, Blades took Don out of the lineup and kept him on the bench for a long stretch. After several days in the dugout, Padgett went to the manager and protested. "How come you're keeping a .400 hitter on the bench?" Don asked. "Because," Blades retorted, "unfortunately you're also a .399 fielder!"

Specialty of the House!

Coach Bill Van Breda Kolff must have been aware that it would not be easy to apply authority to his pro basketball team's new superstar, Wilt Chamberlain, when he joined the Los Angeles Lakers.

Chamberlain, obtained in a trade with the Philadelphia 76-er's, had long been known as a man who cherished his independence. Back in 1963, when Wilt joined the San Francisco Warriors, Coach Alex Hannum was asked how he would handle him. Said Hannum, "I'll treat him the same way I would treat any other 7-foot millionaire who plays basketball!"

Them's Fightin' Words!

When Notre Dame went to Princeton for a football game with the powerful Tigers in 1924, Coach Knute Rockne had such a sore throat he couldn't deliver his usual pre-game oration. The dressing rooms of the two teams, however, were separated by a thin partition through which the Fighting Irish could hear the impassioned speech of Bill Roper, the Princeton coach. Rockne gathered his players close and whispered, "That Roper is giving a great pep talk! Listen to him carefully and pay close attention to every word he says!" Obviously, the Irish listened very attentively — they proceeded to beat Princeton, 12 to 0!

A Game of Inches!

Clifford Shaw was the referee for a football game being played in Austin between the University of Texas and Texas A & M. Texas had moved the ball to A & M's 30-yard line and on their fourth try had carried the attack to within inches of a first down. Shaw called for the chain to make an official measurement, and as he dropped to one knee to get a better view he realized somebody else was helping make the decision.

A small boy had come onto the field and had stretched

himself full length on his stomach with his nose almost touching the ball.

Shaw flattened out on the ground beside the boy, put one arm around his shoulders, and together they studied the situation. After a careful examination and a brief discussion, Shaw and the youngster signalled that Texas had made the first down, and amid the cheers of the fans the boy disappeared triumphantly into the stands!

Send Up a Flare!

One year when Marty Berghammer was managing the old Milwaukee Brewers of the American Association the club was plagued by a prolonged losing streak. Marty finally called a clubhouse meeting before a game and declared, "Today we won't use any signs at all! You've been missing them anyway, so just get out there and do anything you darned please!" The free-lancing Brewers played better than usual, but they still lost. As Berghammer was leaving the clubhouse after the game, an old friend rushed up to him and said profoundly, "You know what your problem was today, Marty? They were stealing your signals!"

Can You Top This?

All golfers have their bad days, but one hapless member of a foursome was having a particularly unfortunate round. On the first 11 holes, he had lost as many balls and was taking a savage beating from par, but his confidence was still brimming over as he stepped up to tee off on the par-3 12th hole. The undaunted duffer gazed out over the scant 180 yards to the green and turned to his caddie. "I should birdie this one easily," he announced, "with a drive and a putt."

He addressed the ball and swung with all his might, barely getting a piece of the ball which trickled a few yards in front of the tee.

"And now," said the caddie, "for one helluva putt!"

Tit for Tat!

"Vinegar Bend" Mizell, a former pitcher who got his nickname from his home town in Alabama, was an unpolished country boy when he joined his first major league club, the St. Louis Cardinals. Mizell was sharp enough even then, however, to get the better of a sophisticated sportswriter who was taunting him.

Mizell had quite a reputation as a singer of country music when he was in the minors. The sportswriter asked "Vinegar Bend" if he was planning a singing career on the stage or in television now that he had arrived in the majors. "Shucks, no," replied the artful pitcher, "I can't sing no better than you can write!"

Life's Little Problems!

George Mikan, who later became the president of the American Basketball Association, was 6 feet 10 inches tall when he reported for freshman basketball at DePaul University in the early 1940's. The freshman coach looked at the towering Mikan and asked George if he had a uniform. Mikan said he had everything but the shoes. The coach said he would dig up a pair of shoes for him and asked George what size he wore. Mikan answered, "Either a 15 or 16." Then George paused, blushing, and added, "But make it size 15, will you? I don't want to look conspicuous."

Charter Member

The Brooklyn Dodgers of the 1920's weren't called the "Daffiness Boys" for nothing. Hardly a day went by without somebody making a costly blunder. Finally, after a long series of particularly stupid mistakes, Manager Wilbert Robinson assembled his players in the dugout before a game and announced that the next man who did anything daffy was going to be fined ten dollars. "In fact," the manager stated, "we're going to have a 'Bonehead Club', and that will be the membership fee — ten dollars!"

Thereupon, Robinson stalked out of the dugout — and instead of giving the umpire his batting order, he handed him his laundry slip!

To Err Is Human . . .

Henry Iba, who coached the United States Olympic basketball team in Mexico City in 1968, won his last collegiate title in 1965 when his Oklahoma State team topped the Big Eight Conference. After the final game of the season, in which the Cowpokes clinched the championship with their victory over Kansas, a reporter pointed out to the happy coach that his team had won in spite of making 19 errors. "Yes, I know," answered Iba, "but it was the possible 20th that worried me most! My boys almost dropped me while they were carrying me off the floor after the game!"

Give and Take!

Clyde Lovellette was understandably proud when he reached the 10,000-point level as a professional basketball player. He was also very pleased when he learned that his teammates of the St. Louis Hawks were planning to give him a trophy to commemorate his accomplishment. Lovellette was surprised, however, when the ceremony started and Coach Paul Seymour began speaking of Clyde's 25,000 points! "It's only 10,000, Coach," Lovellette said modestly. "No," countered Seymour. "This award is for your 25,000 points — the 10,000 you scored . . . and the 15,000 you gave up!"

White Man Speaks with Forked Brogue!

In the early 1900's, Cornelius McGillicuddy, who was later to become better known and beloved as Connie Mack, was a hot-blooded young Irishman just starting his long career with the Philadelphia Athletics. During this time, the club signed a full-blooded American Indian pitcher, who played under the name of Ed Pinnance. Mack, a second-generation Irish import, was then catching for the A's, when a reporter asked Connie for his opinion of Pinnance's ability. The young catcher replied vehemently, "I don't mind tellin' you I've got my reservations about this Indian! As a pitcher, he's fair, but personally speakin', I'm agin' letting all these FOREIGNERS into the game!"

The Eyes Have It!

One of the great football coaches of former times was Bill Alexander, who enjoyed a long and successful career at Georgia Tech. One of Alexander's favorite players was Bill Fincher, a giant tackle who had a glass eye and who was obviously a proponent of psychological warfare. Frequently, in the first few minutes of a game, after Fincher had been involved in violent contact with the lineman opposite him, Bill would slip his glass eye out of the socket and into his hand. Then he would suddenly thrust his face close to his already shaken opponent and growl, "So THAT'S the way you wanna play, huh?"

He Calls 'em as He Sees 'em!

When Leo Durocher was a young shortstop for the St. Louis Cardinals, he recalls a game during which a player on the opposing bench spent most of the afternoon heckling Bill Klem, the veteran umpire. Klem seemed impervious to the barbs, but when Leo came to bat, Bill met him a few feet from the plate and said, "Take a pitch, kid, and see if you can spot the so-and-so who's been yelling at me!" The first pitch sailed in over the plate. Klem called a ball, and Leo started to point with his bat toward the heckler. The umpire immediately dropped all pretense of aloofness. "Don't POINT, you dumb busher," he bellowed, "and that was a STRIKE!"

Offensive Holding!

When Joe Rue was umpiring in the old American Association, he once agreed to try out a newly patented "baseball holder." This wire contraption was shaped like an inner tube, with a trapdoor to release the baseballs. It was worn around the umpire's waist and was designed to hold a dozen balls. Twice, as Rue raced down the third baseline on close plays, the trapdoor fell open, and the game had to be halted while Joe pursued the scattered balls and the fans howled with glee. Finally, as a foul ball and Joe headed toward the grandstand, the trapdoor flew open a third time. Once again the red-necked umpire scrambled — but this time to jerk off and dispose of the offending 'holder'! Joe may have Rue'd the day he agreed to try it, but the device was never seen in a baseball park again!

What's in a Name?

Babe Ruth, during his long reign as the "Sultan of Swat," invariably addressed everyone — even his closest friends — as "Kid." This trait had long bothered Lou Gehrig, Babe's co-star and teammate for 10 years with the Yankees. Finally, Gehrig asked Ruth why he didn't use people's proper names. The Babe explained, "I can't remember names, Kid!" Gehrig insisted he should at least try. "After all," argued Lou, "it's only the polite thing to do. You should realize by now that people appreciate the courtesy of being called by their correct names." Ruth thought it over for a few moments. Then, very earnestly, he gave Lou his answer. "I guess you're right," he stated, "and I'm going to give it a trial, Bill!"

Favorite Son!

Frankie Albert, the former Stanford great who went on to become a professional quarterback, was once the main speaker at a father-and-son banquet. After his prepared speech, Albert volunteered to answer questions from the audience. One youngster raised his hand repeatedly, but somebody else kept beating him to the punch. Finally, the boy managed to get his hand up first. Albert, fully prepared to answer any query concerning passing or tactics, turned to the boy and said, "Alright, sonny. I'm sorry it took so long, but it's your turn at last. What's your question?" Much to Albert's chagrin, the boy stood up and in a loud, clear voice inquired, "What's next on the program?"

Oops!

Because it was such an embarrassing moment, the manager of this American League team shall remain nameless.

After a disastrous start during one of the middle innings, the manager headed for the mound to make a pitching change. Since his relief man hadn't had much time to warm up, he approached the hill slowly, spoke at length to the departing pitcher, and finally walked over to first base and told the umpire to bring in the chosen relief pitcher from the bullpen.

The bullpen, located out of sight in right field, was a considerable distance away, so the umpire set out on his appointed task with dispatch. There was an extremely long delay while the manager, pitcher and some of the infielders stood anxiously gathered on the hill, awaiting the arrival of the new pitcher.

Finally the umpire reappeared. He was obviously irritated as he strode up to the mound and announced sarcastically, "Sir, the pitcher you asked for isn't out there! Which one of the other two would you like brought in?

Last Laugh!

Warren Giles, former president of the National League and a man of many talents, spent most of his professional life in baseball. Yet one of Giles' fondest recollections was a quip he made during a football game.

In his younger days, Giles was a referee for college football, and on the day this incident occurred, he was officiating at a Missouri-Nebraska game. The Nebraska fullback had plunged for what appeared to be a touchdown, but Giles had noted a fumble before the Cornhusker reached the end zone. As he indicated the spot where play would be resumed, Ernie Bearg, the Nebraska coach, ran out bellowing, "How far does a man have to go over the goal line to get a touchdown?" Giles' retort was quick: "With or without the ball, Mr. Bearg?"

Fair Play!

Baseball umpires learn early in professional life that they will always have to put up with a certain amount of abuse — from participants in the game as well as from the fans. It's an occupational hazard none of them can avoid completely, and the only way to cope with it is to stay quick on the verbal draw, maintain a sense of humor and an equally strong sense of timing.

Emmett Ashford, the first Negro umpire in the major leagues, was also one of the sharpest. Knowing a run-in with Leo Durocher was inevitable for any official who came within calling distance of the Lip, Ashford was prepared when Durocher vehemently protested the call on a half-swing. In an effort to appease and quiet him, Emmett walked over to check with the first base umpire, a white man, who concurred in the decision made by his Negro partner.

"So I went back to the plate," recalled Ashford, "and told Durocher: 'There you are. Now you've got the decision in black and white!'"

Butterfingers!

Dick Stuart was one of the leading sluggers in the major leagues for several years. He was also one of the leading fielders at first base — in errors.

Once during the time Stuart was kicking the ball around regularly for the Red Sox, the bat flew out of the hands of the Twins' Tony Oliva and landed near first base. When Stuart picked it up to return it, the Boston crowd applauded wildly.

Later, Dick was asked by a reporter what he thought about the fans' reaction. "Oh, that was nothing," Stuart said. "Once when I was playing for Pittsburgh, I picked up a hot dog wrapper that was blowing around the infield — and they gave me a standing ovation!"

GENE ELSTON, *broadcaster*
for the Houston Astros, has been selected as
sportscaster of the year in Texas by the
National Sportscasters and Sportswriters
Association. This is the fourth time he has
been awarded the honor: in 1965, 1966,
1967 and 1970.
He has been broadcasting for the Houston
Astros and the Colt 45's since 1961.
Previously he was broadcaster for the Chicago
Cubs and later was affiliated with the Mutual
"Game of the Day" broadcast.
Mr. Elston, a native of Fort Dodge, Iowa,
started his career in 1941 broadcasting high
school basketball for Fort Dodge's station KVFD.
His broadcasting experience has brought him
in contact with outstanding personalities
from every area of the sports world.